Japan

in pictures

Prepared by ROBERT V. MASTERS

The Kasumigaseki Building was the first of the new skyscrapers that have changed Tokyo's skyline.

日本

VISUAL
GEOGRAPHY
SERIES

STERLING
PUBLISHING CO., INC. NEW YORK

Oak Tree Press Co., Ltd.
London & Sydney

VISUAL GEOGRAPHY SERIES

Afghanistan
Alaska
Argentina
Australia
Austria
Belgium and Luxembourg
Berlin—East and West
Brazil
Bulgaria
Canada
The Caribbean (English-
   Speaking Islands)
Ceylon (Sri Lanka)
Chile
China
Colombia
Cuba
Czechoslovakia
Denmark
Ecuador
Egypt
England
Ethiopia

Fiji
Finland
France
French Canada
Ghana
Greece
Greenland
Guatemala
Hawaii
Holland
Honduras
Hong Kong
Hungary
Iceland
India
Indonesia
Iran
Iraq
Ireland
Islands of the
   Mediterranean
Israel
Italy

Jamaica
Japan
Kenya
Korea
Kuwait
Lebanon
Liberia
Malawi
Malaysia and Singapore
Mexico
Morocco
Nepal
New Zealand
Norway
Pakistan and Bangladesh
Panama and the Canal
   Zone
Peru
The Philippines
Poland
Portugal
Puerto Rico

Rhodesia
Rumania
Russia
Saudi Arabia
Scotland
South Africa
Spain
Surinam
Sweden
Switzerland
Tahiti and the
   French Islands of
   the Pacific
Taiwan
Tanzania
Thailand
Tunisia
Turkey
Venezuela
Wales
West Germany
Yugoslavia

PICTURE CREDITS

The publishers wish to thank the following people and organizations for the photographs used in this book: Consulate General of Japan, New York; Japan Air Lines; Japan Association for the 1970 World Exposition, New York; Japan Silk Association; Japan Tourist Association; Matsushita Electric Corporation; Pan American World Airways; Yashica Camera Company and Mike Bienstock, T. Mayama, A. Mohri, S. Takano, L. Yanagi, and A. Yoshimoto of that company.

Sixteenth Printing, 1973

Copyright © 1973, 1972, 1970, 1966, 1965, 1961 by Sterling Publishing Co., Inc.
419 Park Avenue South, New York, N.Y. 10016
British edition published by Oak Tree Press Co., Ltd., Nassau, Bahamas
Distributed in Australia and New Zealand by Oak Tree Press Co., Ltd.,
P.O. Box 34, Brickfield Hill, Sydney 2000, N.S.W.
Distributed in the United Kingdom and elsewhere in the British Commonwealth
by Ward Lock Ltd., 116 Baker Street, London W 1
Manufactured in the United States of America
All rights reserved

Library of Congress Catalog Card No.: 60-14338
ISBN 0- 8069–1010–0   UK 7061 6024 X
1011–9

CONTENTS

INDEX

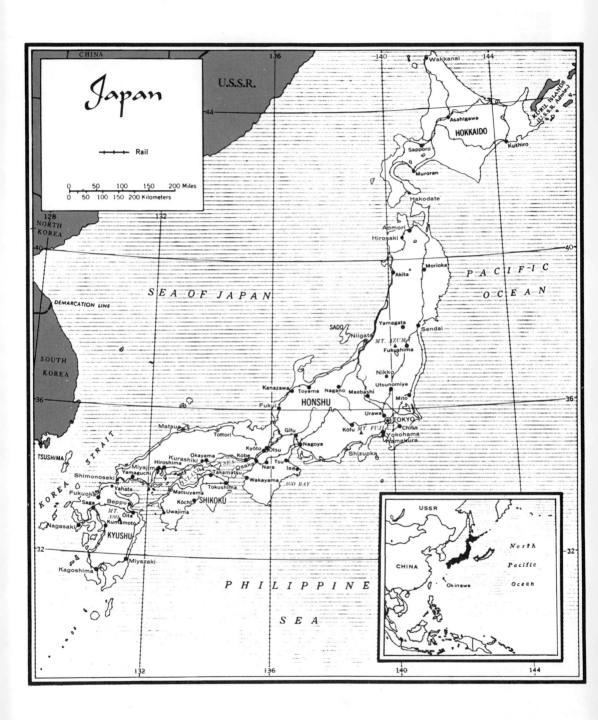

Japan

Rail

| 0 | 50 | 100 | 150 | 200 Miles |
| 0 | 50 | 100 | 150 | 200 Kilometers |

CHINA

U.S.S.R.

NORTH KOREA

DEMARCATION LINE

SOUTH KOREA

SEA OF JAPAN

HOKKAIDO

Wakkanai

Asahigawa

KURIL ISLANDS (U.S.S.R.: Japan.)

Sapporo

Kushiro

Muroran

Hakodate

Aomori

Hirosaki

Akita

Morioka

PACIFIC OCEAN

SADO

Niigata

Yamagata

Sendai

MT. AZUMA

Fukushima

Nikko

Utsunomiya

Kanazawa

Toyama

Nagano

Maebashi

Mito

Fukui

HONSHU

Urawa

TOKYO

Kōfu

MT. FUJI

Chiba

Yokohama

Kamakura

Matsue

Tottori

Gifu

Nagoya

Shizuoka

Kyōto

Ōtsu

Nara

Tsu

Ise

TSUSHIMA

KOREA STRAIT

Kurashiki

Okayama

Kōbe

Ōsaka

Miyajima

Hiroshima

Yamaguchi

Shimonoseki

Takamatsu

Wakayama

AGO BAY

Fukuoka

Yahata

Matsuyama

Tokushima

Saga

Beppu

Kōchi

SHIKOKU

MT. ASO

Ōita

Uwajima

Nagasaki

Kumamoto

KYUSHU

Miyazaki

Kagoshima

PHILIPPINE SEA

USSR

CHINA

North Pacific Ocean

Okinawa

The National Indoor Gymnasium in Tokyo consists of a main building and an annex (left rear). A good example of modern Japanese architecture, the Gymnasium was built for the Olympic Games of 1964.

INTRODUCTION

Unlike most of the other countries of Asia, Japan is firmly at home in the 20th century. It is a modern, prosperous, and highly industrialized nation. Yet in achieving this status, Japan has not turned its back on its own history and traditions. It is an ancient land, and over the centuries it has evolved a uniquely Japanese way of life. One of the most striking features of this way of life is a love of beauty which expresses itself even in the common-places of daily life. The tasteful furnishing of the Japanese home, the practice of elaborate courtesy, the crafting of exquisite pottery and other utensils, the universal writing of poetry, the care lavished on floral arrangement, and the ritual of the famed tea ceremony all attest to this love of beauty.

The elements which make up the Japanese way of life have not all originated in Japan, but have often been borrowed from other cultures and nations. China, for example, has exerted enormous influence on Japanese art, while Western Europe and the United States have been the guiding stars of Japanese economic development, and more recently, of Japanese political development as well.

The mixture of old and new found in most Asian countries is an oft-heard cliché, but one which does not really apply to Japan. For the old and the new are not merely juxta-posed in the landscape of the country, they are interwoven in the life of the nation. The

The past never dies in Japan. Ancient customs and rites are re-enacted in joyous ceremonies like the Festival of the Wild Horse Chase. There are few wild horses around to be caught these days but the chase goes on still.

traditional closeness of the family still prevails, but the Japanese youngster is no longer foredestined as in the past to take up the same occupation as his father and grandfather. Japanese trade unions are constantly achieving economic betterment for the worker, but the employer is still thought of in the traditional way as kindly and fatherly, and often he really is. The Japanese still revere their Emperor, but at the same time they cherish their newly established democracy. With equal enthusiasm they flock to see the ritualistic 14th-century Noh drama, the spectacular 17th-century Kabuki drama, and contemporary Western-style drama. So it goes in nearly every facet of life, for the Japanese seem to have a magic formula for combining yesterday, today and tomorrow. In Japan they are all part of the here and now.

I. HISTORY

Japan can boast one of the world's oldest civilizations. According to myth, the Japanese Empire was founded in 660 B.C. by the Emperor Jimmu. The former Japanese belief that the Emperor was divine stemmed from this myth, which claimed that Jimmu was a descendant of the sun goddess and also the ancestor of all later Japanese emperors. Actually there are no reliable written records of Japanese history prior to A.D. 400, but there is other evidence to show that up until that time, there were many separate tribes and clans inhabiting the country without any national bond among them. One of the clans, the Yamato, managed to assert a rather wobbly supremacy over the others by the 5th century and this was the beginning of national unity.

The Yamato clan strengthened its control over the country during the next three centuries. In 710, the head of the Yamato clan, by then emperor, built a sumptuous capital at Nara. The capital was moved to Kyoto in 794. During the period when Yamato power was being consolidated, Japan was culturally a vassal or subject of China, which was the inspiration for all its art and philosophy. Among the upper classes, Buddhism, a 6th-century import from China, supplanted Shinto, the older and native Japanese religion.

Although the Japanese imperial dynasty is the longest unbroken dynasty in the world, the Japanese emperors throughout history were rarely the actual wielders of power and authority. For long periods they lived in seclusion, sometimes in obscurity, while others—powerful clans or military leaders—ruled in their place. The first such family was the Fujiwara, which gained control of the country by the 9th century. Under them, Japan became a rigidly feudal country and the provincial lords grew in power and prestige. In time rivalries developed among them, erupting in the 12th century into continuous civil wars. By the end of the century, one family, the Minamoto, had succeeded in establishing its supremacy. In 1192 Yoritomo Minamoto, who had taken the title of *shogun*, or military governor, established a new capital at Kamakura. The imperial court, which remained at Kyoto, was totally eclipsed in grandeur and importance by the shogun's court at Kamakura. Yoritomo's descendants became shoguns also, but just as the emperors had lost their power to the shoguns, so too the shoguns eventually lost their power to the members of another clan, the Hojo. The Minamoto were still shoguns but the Hojo family really ruled.

In 1274 and again in 1281 Mongol armies, led by Kublai Khan, invaded Japan but were defeated and pushed back both times.

The shogunate passed into the hands of the Ashikaga family in 1333; five years later they moved the capital back to Kyoto. The Ashikaga had acceded to power through the miscalculations of the Emperor Daigo II. He was responsible for the downfall of the Minamoto régime but he was unable to secure their power for himself. Many civil wars occurred again during the next two centuries, brought on by rivalries among the various feudal lords.

Japan's first contact with Europe occurred in 1542, when Portuguese ships landed in Nagasaki. Seven years later, St. Francis Xavier introduced Christianity into Japan. Further contact with the West was nipped in the bud by Japan's subsequent rulers, and the country was to remain virtually closed to the West from about 1555 to the mid-19th century. Although St. Francis Xavier had gained a foothold for Christianity in Japan, his efforts were largely undone by the official policy of cruelly persecuting Japanese converts.

Three successive military dictatorships were established in Japan in the late 16th century by Oda Nobunaga, Toyotomi Hideyoshi, and Ieyasu Tokugawa. Ieyasu Tokugawa was the founder of a dynasty of shoguns which ruled Japan until 1867. They ruled from the city of Edo (renamed Tokyo in 1868). The Tokugawa shoguns maintained peace and stability in the

7

Old houses in Kurashiki, a city prominent for its many rice granaries during the period of Tokugawa rule.

country, but they did so at the price of economic and social progress. Their rule was repressive and aroused discontent among all the classes of society.

Commodore Matthew C. Perry's landing in Japan in 1854 signalled the coming of great changes in the Japanese Empire. Perry forcibly opened Japan to trade with the Western world, and inevitably this led to other contacts with the West. The glimpses of Western military might and prosperity, together with the realization of Japan's own backwardness and the general discontent which had been growing for years under Tokugawa rule, finally came to a head in 1867. A conspiracy led by nobles of the imperial court and some of the stronger clans of western Japan forced the shogun to abdicate. The Meiji restoration, or accession to power of the Emperor Meiji, occurred in the following year.

The Meiji restoration was a period of intense modernization and Westernization of the country. The foundations of Japan's industrial growth and of the imperialistic expansion which culminated in World War II were laid during the Meiji restoration. The economy of the country was revolutionized, a modern army and navy were built up, and many political reforms were instituted. Japan's first Constitution, modelled after that of Prussia, went into effect in 1889.

Like so many Emperors before him, Meiji, too, was dominated by military cliques, which exploited his prestige to arouse passionate nationalism and blind loyalty among the people.

From 1890 on, Japan embarked on a number of imperialistic ventures, each of which was crowned with success—up until the crushing defeat of World War II. Japan began and won the Sino-Japanese War of 1894-5. The victory brought it control over Korea and the acquisition of new territories—Formosa, the Pescadores Islands and the Liaotung peninsula in Manchuria—but pressure from the West forced it to give up the Liaotung peninsula. Russian challenges to Japanese control of Korea and Manchuria were settled by Japan's victory in the Russo-Japanese War of 1904-5. This triumph over a major European nation won recognition for Japan as a world power. Japan formally annexed Korea in 1910 and made it part of the Japanese Empire.

Japan entered World War I on the side of

Many travellers say that when they go through other parts of the Orient and then land in Tokyo, they feel as if they are back in the West. This district of the city shows why.

the Allies, and after the war it received mandates over the former German island possessions in the Pacific.

Japan's militarism was less active during the next decade. This was a time of enormous economic expansion. The earthquake of 1923, which destroyed nearly all of Tokyo and Yokohama, caused only a temporary setback.

In 1931 Japan resumed its military conquests, subjugating Manchuria and setting up a puppet government there. When the League of Nations censured Japan for this action, Japan withdrew from the League. In 1937

Country villa of one of the Ashikaga shoguns (military rulers), who had it built in 1479. It is sometimes called the Silver Pavilion because the shogun intended to have the whole structure covered with silver, but he never got around to it. Now it is a temple.

Japan invaded the northern provinces of China and set up a puppet government in Nanking three years later. In 1940 it entered the Axis alliance, consisting of Germany, Italy and Japan.

The city of Hiroshima, one of the cities struck by atom bombs, erected this peace memorial after the war.

Japan sparked the entrance of the United States into World War II with its surprise attack on Pearl Harbor in December, 1941. The fact that negotiations between Japan and the United States were going on in Washington, D.C. at the very same time made the attack even more treacherous. During the first two years of the war, Japan seemed to be repeating its habitual military successes, for it gained control of nearly the entire Pacific. The tide began to turn against it, though, in 1943. From then until the end of the war, the United States and its allies slowly but steadily regained control of the Pacific. The intensive bombing of Japanese cities and the disruption of Japanese shipping caused the nation's economy to collapse, but with suicidal fury Japan continued to fight. The dropping of atom bombs on Hiroshima and Nagasaki in August, 1945, finally brought about Japan's unconditional surrender.

When the Allied Occupation began, headed by General Douglas MacArthur, the physical destruction of Japan's major cities, the ruin of its economy, and the thoroughly dispirited morale of its people made it seem that Japan could never rise again to become a strong and prosperous nation. That it did so was due partly to generous economic aid from the United States and to the wise reforms of the Occupation, which served to democratize Japan and liberate the energy of its people. A new constitution went into effect in 1947, and although Japan remained occupied for another five years, it had a great deal of autonomy over its own affairs. It became a sovereign nation again in 1952 and a member of the United Nations in 1956.

In 1968 the United States returned several islands which had been taken from Japan after World War II, including the Bonins and the Volcano Islands. In 1972, the Ryukyus, including the large island of Okinawa, were returned to Japan.

The Jidai Festival of the Heian Shrine in Kyoto is a celebration of the city's ancient glory. One of the most exciting parts of the festival is the procession of people clad in costumes of olden times.

Like all of Japan's cities, the port city of Nagasaki on Kyushu has a long and eventful history. Portuguese sailors landed here in 1542, sowing the seeds of Westernization that bore fruit about three centuries later. Nagasaki was almost entirely destroyed by an atom bomb in 1945. There are few visible scars in the city itself but there are many in the hearts of the people who survived.

11

Nearly all of Japan's many Shinto shrines have entrance gates like the one shown here. Such a gate is called a torii. This one leads to the famous Heian Shrine, built in 1895 to commemorate the 1100th anniversary of the founding of Japan's former capital, Kyoto. Europe was still in the Dark Ages when the resplendent capital of Kyoto was built.

This is where Japan begins for many tourists—the terminal building of Tokyo's modern, bustling International Airport. People land here with eager expectations but often take off with pangs of regret.

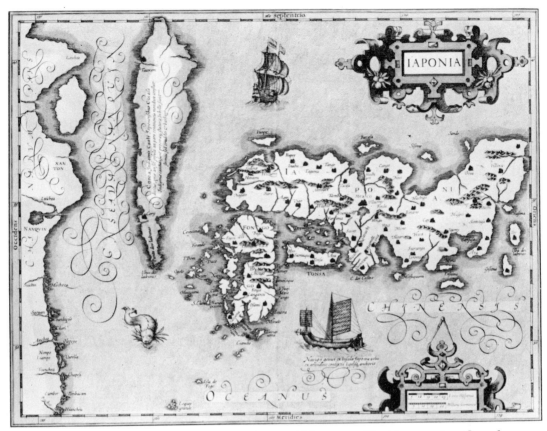

One of the first maps of Japan was by the famous 16th-century Flemish mapmaker, Gerard Mercator. He based it on explorations of the Far East by Portuguese navigators. The map shows only three of the four main islands—Honshu, Shikoku and Kyushu, but not Hokkaido. Korea is mistakenly shown as an island rather than a peninsula of the Asian mainland.

2. THE COUNTRY

Japan consists of a roughly crescent-shaped chain of islands in the northwest Pacific. The chain has a north-to-south span of about 1,300 miles. The total area of the country is about 147,000 square miles. It is about the same size as the state of Montana, although, of course, its shape is very different. Because of Japan's insular nature there is no point in the country that is far distant from the sea. The four main islands are Hokkaido, Honshu, Shikoku and Kyushu. Of the four Honshu is the largest and it contains most of the major cities—Tokyo, Yokohama, Osaka, Kyoto and Kobe. There are also thousands of lesser islands.

A chain of mountains, forming a sort of backbone, runs lengthwise down the middle of all the islands. Mountains are the chief feature of the Japanese landscape. Many of them are extraordinarily beautiful, especially the highest, Mt. Fuji, which rises to 12,397 feet. With its majestic snow-capped peak, it has come to be recognized almost everywhere as a symbol of Japan. Despite the great beauty of the mountains, however, they are economically a disadvantage because most of them are too steep

13

The sea gorge in the Kii Channel between Shikoku and Honshu could probably pass for a Norwegian fiord. The Japanese boat is the telltale giveaway, though.

to be used for farming. As a result Japan has a very small proportion of arable land—chiefly the coastal fringes and a few fairly extensive lowland areas on Hokkaido and Honshu.

Japan has many short, swift rivers coursing down from the mountains. Like the mountains, the rivers are also beautiful, but they subject the country to the ever-present danger of sudden, torrential floods.

Because Japan is situated in a part of the world that is geologically unstable, earthquakes are another form of natural disaster that strikes fairly frequently. The earthquake that destroyed nearly all of Tokyo and Yokohama in 1923 is the most famous in recent history. That earthquake also made famous the Imperial Hotel built by Frank Lloyd Wright—one of the few major buildings in Tokyo that withstood the earthquake intact.

In addition to being picturesque, the Kii Gorge is useful for floating logs downstream.

Volcanic crater on Mt. Aso. There are many romantic tales of desperate lovers flinging themselves into volcanic craters, and many of them are true.

This is Japan's beautiful and beloved Mt. Fuji, located in the midst of a national park southwest of Tokyo. Japanese artists never tire of depicting its lofty snow-capped peak in their paintings. In early Japanese history the people regarded Fujiyama as a sacred mountain.

CLIMATE

Because of the great length of the north-south span of the Japanese islands and because of the great differences in altitude even on the separate islands, the climate varies considerably from place to place. In the north, especially on Hokkaido, the winters are very severe and snowfall is very heavy. Elsewhere winters are milder; the average temperature for Tokyo in January, for example, is 37 degrees. The whole country has hot summers, but the surrounding bodies of water moderate the heat to a great extent and in many places the altitude does too. The average temperature for Tokyo in August is about 79 degrees. The surrounding bodies of water also account for rather high humidity throughout the year.

The annual rainfall varies between 40 and 100 inches. Generally, the western part of Japan, facing the Sea of Japan, receives heavier rainfall than the eastern part. There is a distinct rainy season, usually in August and September. During this season the islands are often lashed by floods and typhoons.

The willow-like cherry tree is one of the loveliest of Japanese trees. It blossoms for only a few days in the spring.

(*Above*) *Shiraito Falls at the foot of Mt. Fuji.*

(*Right*) *This impressive structure is the very modern Sakuma dam.*

(*Left*) *Tokyo's neat modern subway (underground railway) bears comparison with the finest in the West.*

The north-south span of Japan is so long that the vegetation is different at both ends of the country. Palm trees grow on Kyushu, the southernmost of the four main islands.

Japan's scenery is varied enough to suit everybody's taste. The Sahara-like scene shown here is a dune formation near Tottori, Honshu.

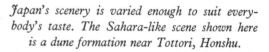

One reason for Tokyo's modern look is that much of the city was destroyed by bombing during the war; most of the rebuilding afterwards was in a very modern style.

One of Tokyo's many narrow side streets, sprinkled with tiny, intriguing shops and restaurants. The street beckons to be explored. Here you can buy objects made of straw, bamboo, rice paper and other inexpensive materials that the Japanese craftsman uses so skilfully and lovingly.

As Japan's busy cities keep growing, so do the traffic problems. Tokyo cab drivers are noted for their nonchalant attitude to life and limb.

The Ginza, one of Tokyo's main thoroughfares. The sound of gay laughter and dance music flows from its elegant modern night clubs. In its many postwar coffee houses, the sedate strains of 18th-century European composers hold teenagers spellbound. Passers-by linger to look at the many chic window displays.

A monorail curves its way through a park in Tokyo.

Except for the electric appliances among the merchandise, Tokyo's side streets have changed little throughout the years.

Here is a shop that handles TV tubes like so many loaves of bread.

3. THE PEOPLE

Japan is one of the world's most densely populated countries. The total population is estimated at about 106,000,000. The density of population is almost 660 persons per square mile. As you would expect, it is a country of many large cities. There are six cities with a population of a million or more: Tokyo-Yokohama (about 11,000,000), Osaka (3,500,000), Nagoya (2,000,000), Kyoto (1,400,000), Kobe (1,250,000), and a city combined from five, Kitakyushu (1,100,000). The total population is still growing.

With the exception of the Ainu people of Hokkaido, the Japanese are almost all of Mongoloid stock. The Ainus are of Caucasoid stock. Most anthropologists believe that the

This young Ainu girl of Hokkaido is dressed in her native costume. The Ainu cling tenaciously to their own habits and customs. They are highly skilled in wood carving.

Ainus were the aboriginal inhabitants of all the Japanese islands and that they were driven to the north by migrations from the Asian mainland of Mongoloid peoples, the ancestors of the modern Japanese people. The Ainus are different in appearance from the Japanese. They remain largely unassimilated and continue to follow their own traditions, which are quite distinct from those of the Japanese proper.

WAY OF LIFE

Many aspects of Japanese life resemble those in any modern industrial nation, but many aspects of it are also quite distinct. Perhaps the most striking feature to Western eyes is the role of the individual in relation to the group. By and large the individual is of lesser importance in the over-all scale of values than he is in the West. More important to the Japanese is the harmonious interworking between the individual and the group, both the family group and the nation as a whole. The individual is expected to discipline whatever traits or desires of his may be in conflict with the group, and from childhood, the Japanese are brought up to understand this. This accounts for the surprising degree of conformity among them and for the elaborate, almost ritual courtesies which govern their social contacts—characteristics which never cease to amaze foreigners.

Differences of social class have become less rigid in recent years but the attitudes that go along with these differences are still evident. There are specific rules of etiquette for contacts between people of different classes. There are even special modes of addressing people of a higher or lower class and special vocabularies to be used in such conversations.

The family is the most important social unit, just as it is everywhere. But in Japan the family is almost clan-like; it includes several generations, not just the immediate family. Family

A common Japanese custom is that of removing shoes before entering a room. Elsewhere in the Orient, people take off their shoes to go into a sacred temple, but only in Japan does the custom apply to homes and Japanese-style hotels too. Here the getas (outer footwear) are arranged neatly so their owners can find them easily when they leave.

loyalty is extremely strong. Members of a family are responsible to one another and are expected to help one another in time of need. A disgrace to one member of the family is held to be a disgrace to all. The head of the family is accorded profound respect, verging on veneration. Indeed, the Japanese respect all old people, even if they belong to a lower social class. Young infants are treated with great affection and do not have to worry much about discipline until they reach an age when they can make themselves useful to the family.

The saving of "face" is extremely important to the Japanese, as it is to most Asians. They often use a "go-between" in situations where they risk loss of face—in marriage negotiations, for example. Many parents still arrange their children's marriages but first they have some-

Typical interior of a Japanese home. To some people the straight geometric patterns and the sparsity of furniture might seem austere, but to the Japanese, the room has an air of purity and serenity unmatched by Western décor.

The sushi *shop is a cross between a Western luncheonette and a Japanese restaurant. Sushi is a popular Japanese dish made of cooked or raw fish, shellfish, eggs, vegetables, and rice flavoured with vinegar and salt.*

Friends get together to enjoy a sukiyaki dinner. Japanese table manners are somewhat different from ours. The Japanese hold up the dish they are eating from with their left hand and take food from it with the chopsticks they hold in their right hand.

(Above) These girls are in training to become geishas. As apprentices, they are known as maiko. *They study dancing, make-up and dress, singing, flower arranging and the ritual tea ceremony. While they are still in the* maiko *stage, they wear a special outfit which includes a distinctive long* obi *(Japanese sash) and* zori *(high-platformed sandals).*

The geisha girls are as lovely as they ever were, even though their training is not quite what it used to be.

one else investigate the history of the other family.

Most of the Japanese have an innate love of beauty and sense of good taste, no matter what their economic or social level. You only have to look at an average Japanese home to see how true this is. The house is usually small and constructed along simple, straight lines. The family uses light, beautifully decorated screens to divide the house into whatever rooms they want at the moment. The rooms do not have permanent furnishings either. Instead, different sets of objects—low tables, cushions, vases, or bedding—are stored in cabinets and placed in

25

A Japanese garden is much more than a patch of ground with straight rows of flowers. It usually includes trees, rocks and a small pool. The apparent look of "naturalness" takes a lot of careful planning.

the rooms for eating, sleeping or entertaining visitors. Exquisitely kept gardens form an integral part of the house; the house is often built around a garden so that people inside can see it from all the windows. Interior décor inspired by Japanese motifs is currently much in vogue in Western countries.

Hardly anyone thinks of Japan without thinking of the geisha girls, and usually what foreigners think of them is incorrect. The word itself means "artist," and, at least in former times, the geisha girls really were artists of the social graces. They were trained for many years in the arts of singing, dancing, conversing, dressing attractively and the like. Their training is shorter and less strict nowadays, but the institution is still very much alive.

On the third or fourth Saturday in July there is a fireworks display around the Ryogoku Bridge in Tokyo. The display has taken place every year for more than two centuries. More recently the display has come to commemorate the American Declaration of Independence and is a token of Japanese friendship towards the United States.

Fishing villages dot the whole length of Japan's long seacoast. Life is very hard in these villages, and the women and children must do their part, too, even though they do not go out to sea.

Small graceful fishing boats anchored near the shore. Like the fishermen themselves, the boats seem to relax and build up strength for tomorrow's busy day. The luckier boat owners have roofs to keep out the hot sun.

Here they are in their almost-naked glory—the sumo *wrestlers. The "referee" looks on in the background. For a while during the Meiji restoration, the Japanese themselves frowned on* sumo *wrestling. They thought it was barbaric and unbecoming for a modern, Westernized nation. Today it is very popular again.*

SPORT AND RECREATION

Wrestling is perhaps the most famous of the traditional Japanese sports, and there are several varieties of it—jiu-jitsu, judo and sumo. Sumo is a kind of wrestling done by professional wrestlers who may charitably be called massive or, more realistically, just plain fat. Three hundred pounds is not an unusual weight for a sumo wrestler. Sumo wrestling bouts are very short; they are over as soon as one man succeeds in throwing the other or pushing him from the ring. There are championship sumo tournaments held three times a year, to the accompaniment of vivid ceremonial pageantry. Unlike jiu-jitsu and judo, sumo is mainly a spectator sport.

Karate and judo are more well known abroad. These forms of wrestling depend less on brute strength than on grace, agility, discipline and quick-wittedness. Judo, although actually useful for self-defense, is cultivated as a sport, beautiful in its precision and elegant in its movements. Karate, similar in some ways, is deadly serious and not merely a sport. Recently, judo has become very popular in the West.

A Japanese entertainer, dressed in a traditional folk costume, amuses guests in a private home.

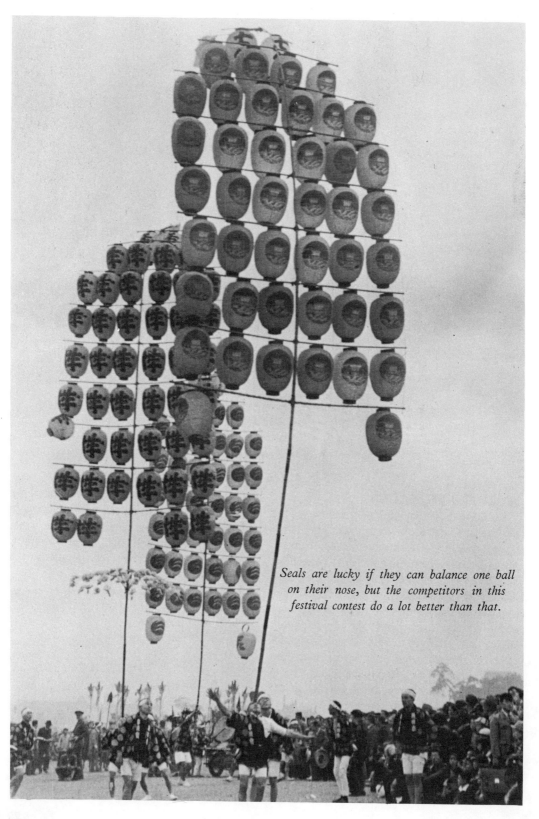

Seals are lucky if they can balance one ball on their nose, but the competitors in this festival contest do a lot better than that.

Tokyo's Kôrakuen stadium attracts as many avid baseball fans as any in America.

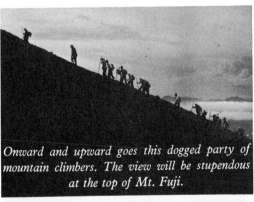

Onward and upward goes this dogged party of mountain climbers. The view will be stupendous at the top of Mt. Fuji.

The Japanese are extremely fond of baseball. Japanese boys love to play it, and throngs of people go to see the professional games. In fact, Japan has its own world championship.

There are plenty of fresh-water streams in Japan for the trout fisherman to choose from.

A girl's basketball team poses earnestly for a group picture.

Like an irresistible magnet, the festival going on below attracts all the apartment dwellers to their balconies. You might think festivals were novel attractions; actually, they go on all the time.

These indoor "pools" are really bathtubs in a Japanese-style hotel on Hokkaido. Bathing alone is considered a bore but bathing in company is a relaxing social event.

Japanese golfers tee off on a three-decker driving range—they are among an estimated 10,000,000 golfers in Japan today. In fact, golf has become such a popular sport that the crowded Japanese landscape barely has room to accommodate all the new golf courses being laid out. New links are being carved out of wooded hillsides, since most of the flat land is used for farming, and ecologists are now issuing warnings about "golf pollution"! Others argue that golf courses preserve greenery that otherwise might be replaced by houses or factories.

Skiing, fishing, mountain climbing, golf or just walking through a beautiful park take up the leisure time of many Japanese. The communal bath is also as much a form of relaxation and recreation as a means of getting clean. Naturally the Japanese also enjoy films, television, nightclubs and all the forms of entertainment that appeal to people the world over.

Some people think shooting the rapids is sport —it all depends on how much taste for adventure you have.

There is always a festival going on somewhere in Japan, with tremendous floats and brilliantly costumed performers.

(*Above*) *Snow may be a nuisance for grown-ups, but it clearly spells paradise for children, no matter where they are or what language they speak.*

(*Left*) *Japan's northernmost main island, Hokkaido, has plenty of ice and snow in winter. When Japan served as host country for the 1972 Winter Olympics, the games were held at Sapporo, the chief city of Hokkaido. Seen here is a trial ski event held just before the actual Olympics.*

The daibutsu, *or bronze statue of Buddha, of Kamakura is seven centuries old. It is 42½ feet high.*

RELIGION

Shintoism and Buddhism are the principal religions of Japan. Unlike Western religions, they are not mutually exclusive and many Japanese consider themselves Shintoists and Buddhists at the same time. Shintoism is in essence a combination of nature- and ancestor-worship. Before and during World War II, Japan's military leaders exploited Shintoism as a means of intensifying nationalistic spirit. It was an effective way of raising loyalty to the Emperor to a fever pitch, since the Emperor, according to Shintoist tradition, was a descendant of the gods. The practice of Shintoism was more a patriotic duty than a religious expression.

Nearly all towns and villages have a Shintoist shrine, and the people hold an annual festival to celebrate the day of the local god's descent from heaven to his earthly shrine. These festivals are joyous affairs, accompanied by

The 50-foot-high torii at Miyajima Shrine rises out of the sea off Miyajima Island, near Hiroshima. It is supposed to welcome the gods of the sea to the island. At low tide people can walk out to the torii and from close up they can see the inscriptions of royalty on its pillars.

A worshipper inside a Buddhist temple.

A huge stone lantern stands between the torii and the Miyajima shrine itself.

This is a famed Buddhist temple at Nara, Japan's first capital. It is called the Todaiji, or Great Eastern Temple. Inside is the daibutsu, or statue of Buddha. Cast over 1200 years ago, it weighs 452 tons and is the largest bronze statue in the world.

communal banquets and drinking, processions and much fanfare.

Buddhism was introduced into Japan from China by way of Korea around the middle of the 6th century. Its acceptance was limited at first to the upper classes, who were prejudiced in favor of any cultural importation from China. By the 13th century people of all levels of society had accepted Buddhism. Many new Buddhist sects arose, although they were still influenced by developments in Chinese Buddhism. Perhaps the best known of these sects in the West is Zen Buddhism.

Buddhism is akin to the many forms of Oriental mysticism which preach a deep sense of communion with all forms of life and with the universe itself, to be achieved only by serene contemplation and by penetrating beneath what appears to be reality. The founder of Buddhism, the Gautama Buddha, is regarded less as a god than as a saint to be imitated. A large body of ethical teaching has grown up around Buddhism. Japanese Buddhism, as practiced today, lacks the zeal found in many other Asian countries with large Buddhist populations. In general, the Buddhist temples

Many families have Buddhist altars in their homes.

are far more elaborate than the Shinto shrines, although many of them are badly attended to and have fallen into disrepair.

A shelf of Shinto tablets is a common sight in many homes.

Graceful prows are part of the pageantry of the Kyoto boat festival.

Members of a school orchestra scraping and tooting for all they are worth.

EDUCATION

Japan has an extremely high rate of literacy. Education is compulsory for all children for nine years, that is, through elementary and lower secondary school. The next stages, if a pupil continues his education, are upper secondary school and then a university. Students are almost automatically promoted from elementary to lower secondary schools, but after that they have to pass examinations to get into upper secondary school and then into a university.

Prior to and during the war, indoctrination was a major aim of education. Schools were supposed to, and did, produce loyal, obedient, highly nationalistic, and well-disciplined subjects of the Emperor. These aspects of education have been dropped altogether. Teaching methods have also become more modern, with greater emphasis on the student's ability to think clearly than just on memorizing facts. Control of the public schools is now less centralized; they are the responsibility of the prefectural (state) governments rather than of the central government.

The traditional snobbishness about different universities has broken down somewhat. The imperial universities, particularly those of Tokyo and Kyoto, are the most highly regarded. Before the war anyone who graduated from either one could be absolutely sure of getting a secure and desirable job as a government functionary. The tendency in the lower schools to concentrate on mere memorization stemmed from this, because it was the ability to parrot back facts that enabled a student to pass the entrance examinations. Since the war many

The television screen seems to have cast a spell over everyone. Educational television is used at all levels of education.

The characters in which Japanese is written are very intricate and hard to learn. It takes a long time to recognize and write them, and to know enough of them to be able to read. Since each character stands for a whole word, you would have to know 10,000 characters to have a reading vocabulary of 10,000 words.

new universities have been founded. They are required to keep up certain academic standards, and qualified graduates of any university can get government jobs. Tokyo and Kyoto Universities still retain their old prestige, but getting into them can no longer make or break the life of the student the way it could in the past.

Scientific research is carried on at many Japanese universities, and Japanese scientists have achieved many notable advances, especially in seismology and nuclear physics. Two Nobel Prizes for physics have been awarded to Japanese scientists. The first was given in 1949 to Hideki Yukawa, a nuclear physicist, and the second in 1965 to Shinichero Tomonaga.

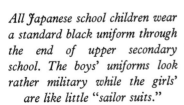

All Japanese school children wear a standard black uniform through the end of upper secondary school. The boys' uniforms look rather military while the girls' are like little "sailor suits."

These typical portraits, with similar poses and even similar facial features, give an idea of the stylization of Japanese art.

4. ART AND LITERATURE

Art plays a less restricted role in the life of the average Japanese than in that of the average Westerner. The ordinary utensils the Japanese use in their homes—the screens, dishes, vases and other objects—and even their traditional clothes, are often minor works of art. The writing of poetry and the practice of calligraphy, or artistic penmanship, are national pastimes.

The Japanese excel in painting, theatre and dance, poetry, architecture, and the making of small decorative objects. Elegance, delicacy and economy of line characterize all the Japanese arts. In painting, the differences between Japanese and Western art are obvious to the eye; they are partly differences in the materials used and partly differences of basic conception. Japanese painting is not done on canvas but on rice paper or silk. The Japanese use fast-drying water paints rather than oils. This means that the artist must execute his painting quickly and faultlessly; he cannot work over it at length. The paintings are not framed. They are mounted on a backing of heavy silk and rolled in scroll form, sometimes up and down, sometimes from right to left.

The differences in basic conception are harder to pin down and it is probably better just to point out some of the ways these differences express themselves. Chiaroscuro (light and shade) and perspective hardly figure at all in Japanese painting, while just plain empty space is much more prominent than in Western art. What the Japanese artist cares about is not merely filling in all the empty space on a piece of paper, but rather suggesting an image by filling in only the barest minimum of empty space. A few deft lines evoke an image by hint and implication. Yet, paradoxically, Japanese painting displays on the whole an infinitely greater love of detail than Western painting.

Although Chinese art has always been a source of inspiration to the Japanese, Japanese art has nevertheless preserved and cultivated distinctive qualities of its own. There have been periods when Chinese influence was stronger than at others, notably the so-called Suiko and Nara periods, dating roughly from the 6th through the 9th centuries. The general trend in the history of Japanese art is pendulum-like,

An artist has just about finished a traditional painting on rice paper. See how much empty space he left. He is working now on the calligraphy, the lettering that so often appears in one corner of a Japanese painting. When he is through, he will mount the painting on a piece of heavy silk.

swinging from periods of almost out-and-out copying of Chinese models to periods of thorough assimilation and transformation of these models. In general, Japanese art has always been somewhat more realistic, more satirical, and more robust in subject matter. A preoccupation with nature is apparent in both Chinese and Japanese painting, but in Japanese painting this preoccupation is less exclusive. Portraiture and genre paintings, that is, scenes depicting everyday life, are also of great importance. The Japanese have achieved special distinction with multicolored prints made from wood blocks.

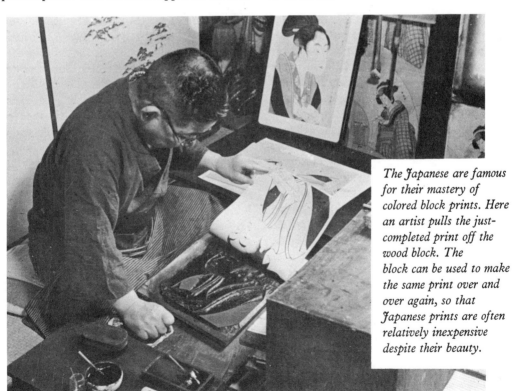

The Japanese are famous for their mastery of colored block prints. Here an artist pulls the just-completed print off the wood block. The block can be used to make the same print over and over again, so that Japanese prints are often relatively inexpensive despite their beauty.

Huge paper lanterns with paintings of legendary heroes are a feature of the autumn festival at Suwa Shrine in Ishiki.

See how finely worked the gold is on the wheels of this festival float. The craftsman must have had infinite patience as well as taste and skill.

In bunraku *the actors who manipulate the puppets are in full view of the audience. This does not bother the Japanese, who never try to pretend that what is going on on the stage is actually happening in real life.*

DRAMA

Traditional Japanese drama is highly stylized and is difficult for the foreigner to appreciate without knowing some of the conventions of the acting and narrating. Japanese drama usually combines drama, dance and music. Often gorgeous costumes, masks and scenery add to the beauty of the whole.

At present the Kabuki drama is the most popular of the traditional forms. Originating in the 17th century as a popular rather than a courtly form of drama, it is essentially a visual spectacle, employing elaborate make-up, costuming, and scenery. Stylized dances are also an extremely important part of the Kabuki drama, which concerns itself less with plot than with stunning performances by the actors; they go in for exaggerated gestures and florid delivery of dialogue. Only male actors participate in Kabuki drama, but actors who take the roles of women use special make-up and gestures.

Interior of a room in the Nijo Castle in Kyoto. The murals, typical of Japanese painting, were done by some of Japan's greatest artists. Notice that one of the squared-off sections is left entirely blank.

43

The Noh drama is another traditional form still popular today. It originated in the 14th century as an aristocratic form of entertainment. Essentially a lyric drama, Noh is more consciously artistic than the Kabuki drama. The dialogue is often highly poetic and symbolic, the scenery is comparatively stark and the actors are masked. Like the Kabuki drama, the Noh drama includes music and dance. In addition it has a chorus, as in Greek drama. Examples of the conventions of acting and narrating in the Noh drama are an actor's raising his hand toward his face to show he is crying or an actor's stamping his foot to show that a ghost has vanished.

The puppet theatre, or *bunraku*, is another theatrical form that has been raised to a high art in Japan. It is really a separate form only in the sense that puppets replace actors. The plays performed are not all exclusively written for the puppet theatre; Noh and Kabuki dramas can also be played with puppets.

Currently, there are also many performances of Western plays in Japanese translation and of original Japanese plays that are Western in style.

A masked actor taking the part of a girl in a Noh play. See how beautiful the brocaded silk costume is.

The Toshogu Shrine at Nikko is an unusually elaborate Shintoist shrine, adorned with brilliant colors and sculpture. The setting is a grove of cryptomeria trees.

OTHER ARTS

Examples of traditional architecture on a grand scale can still be seen in the numerous old Buddhist and Shintoist shrines and the castles throughout the country, especially in the various ex-capitals and in Tokyo. Delicacy and grace mark these structures, built along simple horizontal and vertical lines. The only curves usually are the gentle arcs of the overhanging roofs, sometimes layered one on top of the other. Often the shrines are planned as an integral part of a wooded hillside setting.

(Above) The lion dancer is a much-loved character that appears in many Kabuki plays. His dance consists of wild gyrations that make his "mane" flow in all directions.

(Left) Two girls in traditional dress enjoy the view from part of the lovely Kiyomizu temple, set on a hill overlooking Kyoto.

Close-up of gorgeously costumed bunraku puppets. The man on the left is real.

45

The ancient capital of Kyoto reflects its classic culture even today. One resplendent symbol of its past is the famed Golden Pavilion, built in 1394. Destroyed by fire in 1950, its reconstruction was completed in 1955. Another view is seen on the cover.

This is a graceful floral arrangement of fuji, or Japanese wisteria. Floral arrangements are one of the main features of a room, not just an incidental decoration.

The samisen *is a lute-like instrument, reminiscent of some of the medieval European stringed instruments. Much of the music that accompanies traditional Japanese drama is played on the samisen.*

Kyoto is a veritable museum of the civilization of old Japan. Shown here is the Higashi Honganji temple, a Buddhist temple founded in 1602 and rebuilt in 1895. Like many Buddhist temples, this one consists of a compound of buildings.

These girls, folk dancers from Sado Island, are called Okesa dancers. The ancient steps of their dance are performed to the musical accompaniment of romantic ballads. Their costumes are kimonos.

(Below) The Katsura detached palace in the suburbs of Kyoto was built in the early 17th century. The architect planned the building and the gardens as a whole with the beautiful results you see here.

Examples of the cloisonné ware for which Japanese craftsmen are so justly, famous. They make the design with a network of fine wire and then fill in the spaces with enamel. The word cloisonné comes from a French word meaning "partition" or "membrane."

Japanese craftsmen excel in many minor arts, such as basketry, pottery, porcelain, lacquer, enamel and cloisonné ware, brocaded silks, and damascened swords, which are made of Damascus steel. This is a special kind of steel made by a process that gives it decorative surface patterns.

As in the theatre and painting, Japanese literature at present shows a split between traditional and contemporary Western-oriented forms. The masterpiece of traditional Japanese literature is the *Tale of Genji* by Murasaki Shikibu, a high court lady of the 11th century. The *Tale of Genji*, a long novel about a Don Juan type of Japanese prince, describes court life of the period in great detail.

Poetry has always been one of the most popular forms of literature in Japan. Nearly everybody writes poetry, especially *haiku* and *tanka*, short poems that capture a mood or present one striking image.

The Hirosaki castle in the northern city of Hirosaki is one of the loveliest in Japan. The castle grounds contain luxuriant groves of cherry trees.

Another of Japan's many beautiful and historic castles—this one is in Nagoya.

5. THE ECONOMY

AGRICULTURE

The main staple of the Japanese diet is rice. Rice is the chief crop but the country is not self-sufficient in it. Only about 15 to 20 per cent of the total land area is usable for farming, and this scarcity coupled with the density of the population makes it impossible for Japan to raise all the rice it consumes. Some of the other crops raised are wheat, barley, tea, and fruits and vegetables. Japanese farmers raise very little livestock because they have so little land to spare for pasturage.

All the available land is intensively farmed.

At one time silk was Japan's most important export product. It is still in demand as a luxury item throughout the world. Strange to think that from the silkworm—the rather unattractive creature shown here—will come eventually the fibres that make one of the world's most highly prized fabrics.

These women spend many long hours in the flooded rice paddies of the countryside. Their huge straw hats protect them from the sun.

Fertilizers are used a great deal because the Japanese soil is not naturally fertile. It is further weakened by the necessity of double-cropping, that is, raising two or more crops on one piece of land in the course of one year. As soon as one crop is harvested another is planted so that the land never lies fallow. Most of the farms are very small, only about 2½ acres on the average. Farm machinery is not in widespread use, because it is impractical on such small farms.

The life of the average Japanese farmer is not easy. The raising of rice entails enormous physical work because the land must be terraced and flooded. Usually all the members of a large family help work the farm. The output from such small farms is hardly enough to

The silkworms are not only fussy about where they spin their cocoons but also about what they eat and how much. Mulberry leaves please their palate most. Members of a silkworm farming household carry home basketloads of mulberry leaves from the fields to satisfy the silkworms' gluttonous appetite.

make the farmer rich, despite the fact that the yield per acre is the highest in Asia. Formerly, the life of the farmer was even harder, because so few owned the land they farmed. A system of land reform was instituted, however, after the war under the direction of the Allied Occupation. By now many farmers own their own land and need no longer yield a large percentage of their produce to an absentee landlord.

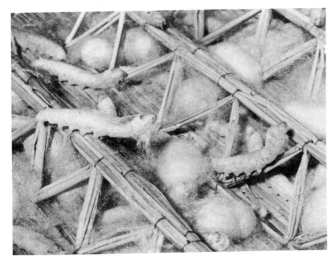

Silkworms are fussy about their living conditions and they have to be pampered if they are to produce silk. The partitioned areas are the individual silkworms' "apartments," in which they spin their cocoons. The whitish balls are cocoons that have already been spun.

In order to utilize mountainous terrain for farming, the Japanese laboriously build terraces up the side of the mountains. Each terrace is a level plot of ground, suitable for growing crops.

Pictures like this of apple-picking in the sun seem so idyllic. The apple-pickers themselves usually say it is backbreaking work.

The box-like contraptions are fishing traps. The fishermen put them in the water, open them and wait for unsuspecting fish to swim in. Then they close the trap on their luckless prey, and bring home the catch.

The Japanese girl pearl divers have been replaced by a cultured pearl industry which developed at the beginning of the 20th century, and has now grown to become one of Japan's leading exports. Japanese scientists discovered just how an oyster covers an inserted "foreign object" (nucleus) with "nacre" (mother-of-pearl). After the nucleus is inserted, the oysters are hung for about three years, from rafts like this one, suspended in sturdy cages. They can then be towed to warmer waters in the winter. When the cages are finally pulled up, the oysters are "harvested" and the pearls removed, sorted, graded, sometimes strung into necklaces or set into brooches, or else sold loose.

FISHING

Fishing is one of the most important activities in the Japanese economy. Fish is the major source of protein in the Japanese diet. Because Japan is surrounded by water, fish is more plentiful than beef or pork and most Japanese prefer it to meat.

Some of the fishing is done by large companies that own extensive fleets, but much of it is done in small family-owned boats that go out on daily or weekly expeditions from the coastal villages. Sardines constitute the major portion of the catch.

Former prides of the sea now lie in the market place, waiting to be bought.

Reconstruction was the first order of the day after World War II. By now, the Japanese have gone far beyond mere rebuilding and are erecting new homes and office buildings that are changing the face of the nation.

Japanese silk is admired all over the world. Here workers dye long bolts of silk according to an old process.

MINING

Mining is relatively unimportant in the Japanese economy because of a scarcity of natural resources. There are many scattered mineral deposits on the islands, chiefly of lead, silver, copper, petroleum, and coal. Only coal is present in anywhere near the amounts needed by the country, and coal mining is a large-scale industry.

MANUFACTURING

In the century since 1860 Japan has transformed itself from a poor, almost wholly agricultural nation into one of the modern industrial giants of the world. This came about partially through a conscious and resolute effort at modernization and partially through sheer economic necessity. Industrialization was essential in order to import food from abroad and to provide adequate employment at home. In the first stages of industrialization, textiles, particularly silk, were the major industrial pro-

ducts. In the 1930's, however, Japan began to turn out large quantities of steel, heavy machinery, chemicals, and electrical equipment, and these industries overtook the textile industry in importance. The war with China in the late 1930's and then World War II spurred the tempo of heavy industrial growth even further.

Despite the fact that the whole Japanese economy was in a state of collapse at the end of World War II, an incredible economic recovery took place in the decade following the war. Technological advances during this period were enormous, partly because higher education was available to so many more people.

Industrial landscapes dot the Japanese countryside. Many of the factories are attractive, modern structures, but even when they are not, the sea or the mountains are always close by to relieve the gloom of the scene.

Economists love and poets decry assembly lines like these. According to the poets, the people look more like machines than the machines do. Somehow, the presence of those flowers in the foreground seems to prove the poets wrong.

Workers assembling television sets. Television is extremely popular in Japan.

At present Japanese industrial production is not only greater in quantity than ever before, but also higher in quality. Japanese precision instruments, such as cameras, microscopes and other optical equipment as well as Japanese electronic apparatus are in great demand throughout the world. The great increase in the Japanese standard of living is traceable to industrialization more than to any other single factor.

Many of Japan's heavy industries and major banks are controlled by the *zaibatsu*, a small number of families that own huge enterprises. The Allied Occupation tried to disband these enterprises and distribute their ownership more widely. After independence, though, the *zaibatsu* regained their former economic power, only slightly diminished.

No place for flowers on this busy assembly line.

The level of Japanese technology is very high. Japan's skilled workers are noted, too, for the excellence of their work, a carry-over perhaps from the long tradition of skilled craftsmanship. Another factor in Japan's high productivity is the good relationship between workers and management throughout Japanese industry. Benefits to workers are considerable, and strikes are rare.

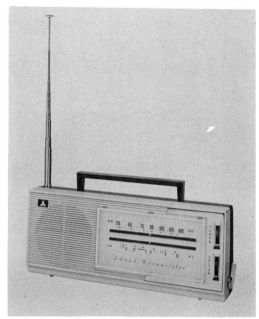

(Left) This is not the Eiffel Tower in Paris! It is a television tower in Tokyo. An elevator goes up through the middle to an observation platform. There, from a height of 400 feet, people can see out over the whole city.

(Above) Sleek streamlined Japanese transistor radios are also of high quality. Items like these are changing Japan's international trade reputation. Before the war, when people thought of Japanese exports—apart from silk—they thought mostly of cheap souvenirs and gewgaws, but now they are more likely to think of high-quality, well-designed precision products.

TRADE

Perhaps more than in any other country, the prosperity of Japan's economy depends on foreign trade. The most important reasons behind the necessity to export are the need to buy foodstuffs abroad, the need to import raw materials since Japan has so few natural resources of its own, and the fact that, despite its large population and increasing standard of living, Japan still cannot supply a large enough domestic market for the consumption of its own industrial products.

One of the obstacles to Japan's export of industrial products is the high cost of transportation to distant markets, such as Western Europe. However, by 1973 other Asian nations, were becoming major industrial markets. Another obstacle is the high cost of Japanese industrial production, due in part to the importation of raw materials. To some extent this can be offset by low wage costs, but Japanese trade unions are becoming more and more powerful with the result that wage costs are rising steadily. When the Japanese do succeed in exporting products at a competitive price, the consequence often is the clamping down of protective restrictions by the country they exported to. The United States, for example, has high protective tariffs on certain Japanese

Japanese cameras are an important export product. They are less expensive than other nations' cameras, and many photographers, both amateur and professional, say they are just as good if not better than American and European makes.

goods. Nevertheless, the United States is Japan's largest customer, absorbing about a quarter of its total exports.

The main long-range solution to Japan's export dilemma would appear to be large-scale trade with Communist China because of its proximity and its need for industrial products to nurture its own rapid industrial growth. In the meantime the growing dependence of other parts of eastern Asia on Japanese imports is helping to bridge the gap. In 1973, the Philippines, Taiwan and South Korea relied on Japan for nearly half their imports, Thailand for one third, and Indonesia for one fourth.

SHIPBUILDING

The majority of Japan's exports are products of the heavy and chemical industries. Perhaps the most dramatic growth has been in the ship-building industry. Most Westerners do not realize it, but Japan is the world leader in ship-building, with more than four times the production of the second-place country, Sweden. Low costs have enabled the Japanese to sell ships to nearly every country in the world, and they are producing some of the largest ships ever built, too.

Japan entered the 1970's as the third greatest economic power in the world, replacing

The "Tokyo Maru" was the largest tanker in the world when launched in January, 1966. By August of that year it was already surpassed by another Japanese-built tanker, however, and even larger tankers were already under construction.

Seen from the air, the Japanese Government Pavilion (foreground) at Osaka's 1970 Exposition looks like a cluster of birthday cakes. The fair was indeed something to celebrate—for it broke all attendance records for a one-season world exposition.

West Germany and outranked only by the United States and Russia. By 1969, the Japanese standard of living was as high as that of many Western countries. Television sets, refrigerators, electric rice cookers and washing machines are now commonplace. Along with prosperity have come problems, for more and more people are moving to the cities, where there is not enough housing for them. The strong family ties of the Japanese are showing signs of weakening—young city people are now more inclined to follow a career of their own choosing, live where they please and marry without their parents' approval. Traffic jams and overcrowded apartments are still common in spite of new high-rise buildings and improved highways and public transport. But the Japanese are generally confident in their future, and of their ability to use their economic power for peaceful development.

The motto of the 1970 Osaka world fair—Expo '70–was "Progress and Harmony for Mankind."

At opening of Expo '70.

6. GOVERNMENT

The Crown Prince and his bride in court robes for their wedding ceremony. Only the wedding couple and a Shinto priest were present at the ceremony itself.

Before and during the war, Japan had the outer political trappings of democracy, but the parliament was too weak to be effective, political liberties were suppressed by a strong, nationally controlled police force, and the leaders of Japan's military establishment had more authority in practice than the civil government. The Emperor, though not in actual control of the government, was in theory the ultimate sovereign power. Whether or not he personally approved of the militaristic policies that led Japan into war is open to question, but there is no doubt that he was the emotional symbol that imbued the nation with a suicidal will to conquer.

The most striking change in the Japanese political system is the emergence of a working democracy, based on universal suffrage. Under the new Constitution, which went into effect in 1947, Japan has a parliamentary form of government similar to that of Great Britain. The parliament, known as the Diet, has two houses, the House of Councillors and the House of Representatives. The lower house, the House of Representatives, is the stronger of the two. It elects the Prime Minister from among its own members and the Prime Minister is then responsible to it. One of the most extraordinary features of the new Constitution is an article that expressly renounces war and forbids the maintenance of a large military force.

In 1946 the Emperor publicly denied his own

Crown Prince Akihito and his bride, Michiko Shoda, daughter of a wealthy businessman, ride in the imperial horse-drawn carriage to their wedding. Most of the nation rejoiced over their wedding, but the ride to the ceremony was marred by an attempted attack on the Prince from someone in the watching crowds.

divinity. Now he is a figurehead and his functions, like those of the Queen of England, are ceremonial rather than political. Crown Prince Akihito's 1959 marriage to a commoner gives an idea of the changed status of the Emperor and the imperial family. Such a marriage could never have taken place in prewar Japan.

(Below) Crown Prince Akihito and Crown Princess Michiko with the Emperor and Empress, who received them in a ceremonial audience following the wedding ceremony.

The National Diet Building in Tokyo, located on a hill near Hibiya Park. The building has an imposing dignity which members of the Diet often lack. They are notorious for starting fist fights during sessions of the Diet.

POLITICS AND FOREIGN RELATIONS

Japan's two major political parties are the Liberal-Democratic party and the Socialist party; the latter contains both a Marxist faction and a less radical faction resembling the British Labour party. The Liberal-Democratic party has been consistently stronger and is currently in power. In addition to its economically conservative policies, the Liberal-Democratic party supports Japan's alignment with the West and, more specifically, the mutual defence treaty between Japan and the United States. Among the reasons for supporting the treaty are that ideologically Japan is drawn towards the free world; that economically it needs the United States, which is its biggest customer; and that, without a strong military force of its own, and situated so close to the Soviet Union and Communist China, it also needs the United States for defence.

The Socialists want a neutral course for Japan and advocate breaking the treaty with the United States. Even though the Socialists are not in control of the government, their neutralist and pacifist policies find a good deal of sympathy among the Japanese people. As the only victims in wartime of the atom bomb, the Japanese are particularly fearful of a third

This round tower of glass is a new office building in the heart of Tokyo. Since the government lifted restrictions on the height of buildings, there has been a building boom.

63

Located in the middle of Tokyo, the traditional-style Imperial Palace, with its spacious grounds and encircling moat, is like an enclave from the past lying right at the heart of the present.

world war in which nuclear weapons would probably be used, and they are afraid of being drawn into such a war willy-nilly because of their alliance with the United States. In addition many Japanese feel that eventually they must turn to Communist China for trade, and traditionally the country has always gravitated culturally towards China. All these sentiments are exploited to the utmost, not only by the Socialists, but also by the Japanese Communist party which is small, but well-disciplined and effective. With its great industrial might and its large population, Japan is a prize the Communists would very much like to ensnare in their own camp or at least detach from the West, and they are not likely to spare any effort to achieve these ends.

Three 1971 developments have had considerable impact on Japanese opinion and will affect future Japanese policy. In that year, Communist China was admitted to the United Nations, an event that the Japanese had expected to take place eventually.

Then, President Nixon of the United States accepted the invitation of Chou En-lai to visit Communist China, breaking the ice after 21 years of mutual distrust. Also in 1971, the United States lifted its embargo against trade with mainland China. In February, 1972, President Nixon visited China, where he was cordially received. For the political and economic life of Japan, a new era had begun.